# Beyond Repair

## Lois Peterson

*Orca currents*

ORCA BOOK PUBLISHERS

**Library and Archives Canada Cataloguing in Publication**

Peterson, Lois J., 1952-
Beyond repair / Lois Peterson.
(Orca currents)

Issued also in electronic formats.
ISBN 978-1-55469-817-2 (bound).--ISBN 978-1-55469-816-5 (pbk.)

I. Title.  II. Series: Orca currents
PS8631.E832B49 2011      JC813'.6      C2010-907995-7

First published in the United States, 2011
**Library of Congress Control Number:** 2010942100

**Summary:** Cam, still grieving over the death of his father,
is worried that he is being stalked.

MIX
Paper from
responsible sources
FSC® C016245
www.fsc.org

*Orca Book Publishers is dedicated to preserving the environment and has printed this
book on paper certified by the Forest Stewardship Council.*

Orca Book Publishers gratefully acknowledges the support for its
publishing programs provided by the following agencies: the Government
of Canada through the Canada Book Fund and the Canada Council for the Arts,
and the Province of British Columbia through the BC Arts Council
and the Book Publishing Tax Credit.

10% of the author royalties of *Beyond Repair* will be donated to youth programs at
the White Rock Hospice Society

Cover design by Teresa Bubela
Cover photography by Dreamstime

ORCA BOOK PUBLISHERS
PO Box 5626, Stn. B
Victoria, BC Canada
V8R 6S4

ORCA BOOK PUBLISHERS
PO Box 468
Custer, WA USA
98240-0468

www.orcabook.com
Printed and bound in Canada.

14  13  12  11  •  4  3  2  1

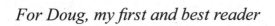

*For Doug, my first and best reader*

# Chapter One

Even from my bed, I can tell it has snowed outside. All around is a soft silence.

But not for long. "Cam?" Leah thumps on my door.

"Buzz off."

"Cameron!"

"Okay, okay. Come in if you must."

In the morning my sister always looks much younger than seven. She is fresh and clean, and her tantrums from the day before have washed away.

I sometimes wish I could get away with her hissy fits. I'd love to dump my cereal bowl on the floor just because we're out of Shreddies.

Mom keeps threatening to take Leah to a psychologist. I don't get to freak out. Too many people telling me, "Your mother and sister depend on you. You're the man of the house now."

Real men don't throw cereal bowls.

"Can I come in?" Leah stands in the doorway in her purple jammies.

"You're in, aren't you?"

"I'm hungry." She walks to my bed and shoves her face into mine. She runs her finger across my top lip. "You're getting a mustache!"

I leap out of bed and peer into my mirror. I tip my head one way, then the other. There is a glimmer of hair above my lip. If I wasn't so fair, I'd have been shaving months ago, like my best friend DJ.

"You could have Dad's razor," says Leah. "If Mom hadn't thrown it out."

When she starts to snivel, I do the only thing that can stop her. "Snap out if it!" I yell. "Or you'll make me cry too."

"You're mean. It's okay to cry." She rolls her bottom lip up over her top lip and sticks out her tongue to lick the snot creeping toward her mouth.

"Don't do that. It's disgusting. And you don't have to cry every time someone mentions him."

"What's that noise?" Leah asks. She climbs on my bed and pushes the curtain aside. "It's snowing!" she screeches. She bounces back down. "Let's get dressed so we can go out in it."

"We've got school. Anyway, it won't last."

"I want to stay home and play in the snow." Leah's already headed to her bedroom. "If we're out there when Mom gets home, she can't stop us."

*Wanna bet*? When Mom gets back from her night shift at the hospital, she expects to find us dressed and eating breakfast, with our lunches packed. Some days she's so tired, she can hardly say hello before she heads to her room, still in her coat.

I look outside. Then I lean closer. So close I can feel the cool air on the other side of the window. It can't have been snowing that long. There's hardly enough to shovel.

But someone is out there already. And the driveway being shoveled is ours.

The shoveler is wearing a green parka with the hood pulled up. It's not Mr. Lyon from next door. He has emphysema. Our neighbors on the other side are in Disneyland with their four kids.

I pull on a sweatshirt and drag yesterday's pants over yesterday's underwear. I hop across the room, first on one leg, then on the other, as I pull on yesterday's socks.

Leah is sitting in the middle of the hallway struggling into her snowsuit. "Hurry up," she says. She frowns down at her zipper. "I wanna make a snowman."

"Idiot. There's not enough snow. Anyway, you've grown out of that." As I push past her, I hear the muffler on Mom's car. It's been growling for six months. I can hear it from a block away. "Mom will be here in a minute. Quick. Get to the table."

Leah trails after me into the kitchen with the top half of her snowsuit dragging behind her. "Can we have French toast?" she asks.

"It's not Sunday."

"If Dad was here, he'd make me French toast if I asked."

*Oh, sure he would!* I think. *Just like he'd help you do your homework or fix your bike.*

"I don't want French toast really," says Leah. "You make it all sloppy."

"Quit jabbering on about it, would you!" I say. Can it be possible that she's a bigger pest now than ever?

"I want Mommy," she whines. She struggles out of the snowsuit and drops it in a pink puddle by her chair.

"Stuff it, will you." I set out a box of cereal and a jug of milk in front of my whiny sister.

"You're mean," she wails. "You're the worstest brother in the world."

"It's *worst*. Not *worstest*. Eat your breakfast." I go into the living room and pull back the curtains.

Outside, Mom is standing on the driveway. There's some snow on the ground, but hardly enough to stop traffic—or to need clearing yet.

She's yelling at a man who is leaning on a shovel. She's probably mad because the shovel is making a great gouge in her daffodil bed. As she waves her arms, her purse swings to and fro. When it hits the man's leg, he moves aside. Then he leans toward Mom, talking right into her face.

He holds up one hand. He's keeping Mom back, or calming her down. I can't tell from here.

I can only make out a bit of what she's saying. "You have no business…!" she yells. "I'll report you. If I catch you…"

The man steps closer, as if he's begging.

*Let him go*, I think. *They're only flowers, for Pete's sake.*

Mom turns her back on him and heads for the house. As she flings open the front door and rushes inside, a gust of cold air swirls into the room. The door slams behind her.

Her face is very pale. Her eyelashes glisten with tears. She's breathing hard.

"What was that about?" I ask. "Who is that?

She takes a deep breath in, then lets it shudder out of her as she stares through me. She opens her mouth, but no words come out. Tears wash down her face.

She takes another ragged breath. "That…" She waves toward the front door and gulps. "That's the man who killed your father."

I rush back to the window. "What? What do you mean?"

All I see are exhaust fumes as a blue pickup disappears from sight—and a snow shovel sticking out of my mother's favorite flower bed.

## Chapter Two

It takes me a while, but I finally manage to get Leah out of the house and dropped off at school.

I've never seen Mom quite so riled. She was a savage mixture of mad and desperate as she stomped around the kitchen. I was glad to get out of there.

"Talk about spooky," says DJ when I tell him who showed up. "That guy must be some kind of creep." He slaps his locker door shut and it flips open again. "He really said he was helping out? Just doing what your old man would be doing if he was still here?" He slams the locker shut again. It bounces back.

"You ever see Dad shovel a driveway?" I ask. Like DJ—or anyone—ever saw my father do anything that didn't involve the financial pages of the newspaper or computer spreadsheets. I doubt he even knew how to use a shovel.

"And we'd have run him off soon enough, wouldn't we?" DJ grins and slams the locker door one more time. It finally closes.

After a big snow last winter, DJ and I roamed the neighborhood offering to shovel people's driveways. For free. He figured that if we didn't ask for payment, people would be so grateful, they'd give us more than they would if we set a price.

It worked.

Most people gave us ten or fifteen bucks when I thought the job was worth five, maybe ten for very long driveways. One woman even gave us a fifty-dollar bill. She wouldn't take any change. Later, on my way home, I shoved a twenty in her mailbox.

I didn't tell DJ though. He'd think I was soft.

Even better than the hundred and eighty bucks I made that day was that, when I got home, wiped out and freezing, Dad was actually there. He set his stacks of papers aside and turned off the computer. He even made me tomato soup and a bologna sandwich. And he sat at the kitchen table with me while I ate it. It was some kind of a first. I knew better than to make a big deal of it. I just ate slowly to make it last. We talked—although I can't remember what about.

"What do you think I should do?" I ask DJ.

"What's *to* do?" he asks. "The guy wants to shovel your driveway. Your mom sends him away. End of story."

"What if he comes back?"

"Want me to deal with him?" DJ asks.

"Like how?"

"I dunno. Put sugar in his gas tank. Graffiti his house. You do know who he is, right?"

"Yeah," I say. That is not something I'd forget. The man's name was all over the paper for a couple of days after the inquest.

DJ pushes off from the locker and heads down the hall. "That's settled then. Next time he bothers you or your mom, you tell me. I'll sort him out." He flexes a puny arm.

DJ talks like a tough guy. He's the biggest chicken I know. And he knows it.

So we're both laughing when we head into homeroom.

Sad Sack Stacie in her weird clothes looks up at DJ. "What's so funny?" she asks.

DJ thinks Stacie has a crush on me. I hope she has a crush on him.

"Did you know the Inuit have a thousand words for snow?" he asks her. She yanks up her tights by dragging on her plaid skirt. Very classy. Her tights are yellow. Her skirt is short. Very short. Like I'd notice.

She nods. "Actually, that's an urban myth. It's not that they have so many words. It's just that they have so many dialects."

That stuns DJ for a second. But he recovers quickly, shakes his head and walks away. "I asked for that," he mutters as we head for our seats. "Didn't I ask for that?"

"Mom says that the guy showing up on our driveway amounts to stalking," I tell DJ. "It's even spookier when I think of it like that."

"What would you do if you ran into him?" he asks.

"Punch him." It's a stupid thing to say. I've never hit anyone in my life—at least not since I was Leah's age.

I'm the man of the house now. My grandparents, aunts, Mom's friends are always saying that. I'm supposed to fix things and take care of everyone. I thought they meant grocery shopping and helping Leah with her homework. I can do that. It's not like it's any different than when Dad was alive.

But now am I supposed to chase off this guy too?

"So you tell me," I say. "What would *you* do if the guy who killed your father showed up and wanted to help around the house?"

"I'd invite him in. Trade my old man in for the new model." DJ's father is always on his case. About his schoolwork—Bs aren't good enough. His girlfriends—he hasn't got any. His hair—it's never combed.

At least his dad notices this stuff.

What *would* I do if the guy showed up again? I wonder.

Bryan Klausen, 43. A millwright. What's a millwright? Klausen is a family man with two kids and a wife who teaches social studies. Not at my school, that would be too spooky.

I already know too much about this guy from the article about the inquest. No one knows I keep all the newspaper clippings under my bed.

# Chapter Three

"Hey, Cameron," says Stacie a few days later when I get to work. It is ten after five. I'm late thanks to Leah. She made a big fuss when I dumped her at the sitter's. Thankfully, Marcus the Midget Manager is not around.

"You're on returns," Stacie says. "I covered for you."

I mutter, "Thanks."

When I head for the drop box, she's right behind me. "I bet working helps out at home," she says. "Like, now that your mom's the breadwinner."

"My dad was insured." As soon as it's out of my mouth, I know it's a dumb thing to say. But my mouth often moves before my brain's in gear. "And my mom's a nurse. You know how much they make these days. Hey, maybe you could be a nurse when you grow up. Oh, wait—you need good grades for that."

I can tell by her face I've gone too far. She turns away and slinks off.

Jeez. A couple of months ago, I'd never have been so mean.

I drag the returned movies out of the box, cracking my head as I back out to pile them on the cart.

"Is that what you call a uniform?" The Midget Manager is in my face, breathing licorice fumes at me. He lives on red Twizzlers that I bet he doesn't pay for.

I look down at my pants and Oilers sweatshirt. I've forgotten to put on my work shirt. Smocks, they call them here. It's a stupid name for stupid clothing. "Oops." I fake a laugh. "I'll head right back to the staff room and put it on."

"You do that. After you've taken care of these." He gives the cart a shove.

I'm about to do just that when he says, "And one more thing."

"Yes, Marcus."

"I know it's been tough. Your dad and all. And I've made allowances."

I try to edge past him, but he takes a step sideways so he's blocking my way. "You've had breaks no one else gets," he goes on. "I give you shifts that work with your mom's schedule. Overlook lateness. But it can't go on forever. You're part of a team. We all pull together."

This sounds like something he heard at one of the managers' team meetings he's always going to.

Then he adds, "Don't think I don't know how tough things are for you."

I stare at the DVDs jumbled on the top shelf of the cart. I've learned that it's best to avoid eye contact with people who feel sorry for you. Even mini-twits like Marcus.

"But I expect you to be on time for your shifts from now on," he says, all business again. "Wear your uniform. And don't upset the other staff."

Either Sad Sack Stacie's been telling tales. Or our great leader *has* been keeping tabs on me, despite his phony compassionate pitch.

"*Capiche?*" He taps his pen against his teeth.

"*Oui, monsieur*. Is that all?" *Capiche*? Someone should tell him that

Canada's second language is French. Not Spanish. Or Italian. Whatever that was.

When he stands aside to let me pass, I push through the swinging door that separates the customers from the checkout counter.

I decide to make nice with Stacie. Even the unpopular girls at school don't include her in their airhead talk about nail polish and *The Bachelor*. And there's not a guy in his right mind who would make a pass at her. Could be something to do with the short, short skirts. And the tights. Today they are green.

I hold up a copy of *Lip Sync*. "Seen this?" I ask her. "It must be new."

"It came in weeks ago." She rings up chips and pop for a mom with about eight kids scrabbling around her. "Would you like a bag?" she asks the customer.

Even though the woman says no, Stacie shoves her videos and snacks into a bag and passes it across the counter.

How's that for customer service?

She starts handing me movies off the cart so I can check them in. "You're supposed to know the stock," she says in a prim voice. Then, in case I've forgotten, she adds, "I recommended you for this job, remember. I'm going to look stupid if it doesn't work out."

You'd have thought she saved me from an icy death in the Fraser River. Not just gave me the lead on a lousy job at Video Mart, which she won't let me forget for a minute.

I'm saved from any more lectures by a customer leaning across the counter. "Excuse me. I'm looking for a copy of *Hamlet*."

"I can look that up for you." Employee of the Year Stacie puts down the stack of movies she's holding. She turns to the computer. "There's a number of versions. I'll see what's in."

"Oh. I don't want to trouble you," says the guy. "You look busy. But perhaps this young man can help me. But thank you"—he leans forward and reads the name tag on her flat chest— "Stacie, is it? Thank you."

"It's no trouble at all." She moves to the computer and types madly. Before he can say anything else, she taps the screen, "Classics. Is the one with Kenneth Branagh in it the one you want? Or Mel Gibson? Let me show you."

The man looks back at me once as he follows her across the store.

Something about the way he walks… I can't quite place it, but he seems familiar. When he glances back at me, I look down and get busy separating the comedies from the dramas.

"Now that was weird," says Stacie when she comes back.

"Weird how?" I ask.

"The movie he wanted was right on the shelf. But he didn't even pick it up."

"Happens all the time," I tell her. "Folks come in wanting one thing and find something better. Sometimes something recommended by people like you. Who know the stock." I can't help making the dig.

It's like she doesn't hear me. She taps *Finding Nemo* against her chin and looks toward the big picture window smothered with posters. "Like, he just said thanks. Then took off." She slips the movie in among the stack of others waiting to go out on the floor. "But first he asked your name," she says. "Like you weren't wearing a name tag. Oh. You're not."

I ignore the superior look spreading across her face and look toward the door.

A chill creeps across my shoulders. Now I remember that walk.

I remember the quiet of that day it snowed. The harsh sound of the shovel on the driveway. The guy walking to his truck after my mom was finished yelling at him.

Stacie is blathering on about privacy and store policy as I shove past her. She gives a little squeak when I tread on her foot.

I barge through the doorway past a skinny punk and his girlfriend who are on their way in.

I scan the sidewalk and the parking lot.

I can't see the guy anywhere. I hang on to the door handle, feeling its cold edge cut into my palm.

The guy's gone.

Mom said she would report him to the police if he showed up at the house again. But I bet she'd never thought he'd turn up at my work.

But that was him. I know it.

Which, in my book, makes him a stalker.

## Chapter Four

DJ sits on my bedroom floor with his back against the bed. He throws a yellow tennis ball against the door. Good thing Mom's at work. She'd be on my case about the noise in a flash.

"I can see why you'd be freaked out, dude," he says as the ball lands back in his hand. "What say we turn the tables on the guy?"

"Turn the tables how?"

"Give the guy a piece of his own medicine."

"Taste. It's a taste of medicine," I say. "You're mixing metaphors."

"Thanks, Mr. Shakespeare. Taste then," he says. "How about this? We follow him."

"That makes us as bad as him, doesn't it? Mom called it stalking when he showed up here. It's stalking when he tracks me down at work. So it's stalking if we follow him."

"What I'm planning is called a stake-out. Stalking! Your old lady is a drama queen. So the guy wants to shovel your driveway. Pick up a movie or two. Doesn't make it stalking."

"Feels spooky though."

"That's because you have no curiosity. Why he would want to come within a hundred miles of you and your mom is what I wonder."

"Me too."

"So let's check him out." DJ reaches out to catch the ball, but this time he misses. "Suss out what he wants," he adds, as he watches the ball roll under my bed.

"Leave it," I tell him.

He bends down to peer at the crap I know is there. Lost underwear. Candy wrappers. The manila folder I took from Dad's desk. "It's no big deal," I tell him. I've got another ball somewhere."

Ignoring me, he kneels down with his butt in the air. I hold my breath as he sticks his arm under the bed and gropes around. He comes back up right away holding a cobwebby balled-up sock, a couple of pencils and a CD.

I grab for the CD with relief. "What's that?"

"Raffi."

"Shove it back quick. Leah's been on about it for months. I swore up and down I didn't have it."

Dust flies off the jewel case as he slaps it against his knee. "That Leah's a nice kid," he says. As if that has anything to do with anything. He throws the CD on my bed, and as he gets up he chucks the sock at the wall. It just rolls down and falls to the floor. "So, you wanna check out the guy?"

"How are we going to do that?" I ask.

"So obvious." DJ shoves me out of my desk chair, sits down and starts typing. "Canada411," he says as his hands hover over the keyboard. "Let's get his address to start with. Phone number, too, would help. What's his name?"

When I don't say anything, he looks up at me. "Well?"

"I know it. Course I do," I tell him. I knew the guy's name the other day. But right now it's like everything in my head is erased.

"I should know it too," says DJ. "I read it in the paper." He lowers his voice. "It's weird. Reading about someone you know. Especially when the guy… you know the person it talks about is…"

"The dad of a friend of yours? Is that what you're after? Or do you mean dead?"

He gives a mock shiver as he turns back at the monitor. "Gave me the chills. So. The guy's name?"

Maybe it's psychoso…psycho-somatic. The memory loss. I knew the name of the guy who drove over my father like he was just a little bug. But I can't remember it. I must have blacked it out. There's a term for it—selective something. Selective amnesia. That's it.

There are a lot of other things I wish I'd blacked out. Hearing the news. Waiting in the cold hallway at the morgue while my mom had to... Standing in a huddle in the pouring rain at the cemetery. I thought funerals held under dripping black umbrellas only happened in the movies.

I slump onto my bed.

DJ turns around to look at me. "Hey, dude. We need the name."

I lie back and stare at the ceiling. I swipe my arm across my face. But the tears keep coming. I try to take a breath. "I know it. I know I do. But I can't remember."

"Shit, man." DJ is looking in my direction, but not at me. His legs bounce up and down, so I know I'm making him nervous. Last time he saw me cry was in elementary school. I had wiped out on my bike after I tried to ride it down the playground slide. Don't try that at home.

"I've forgotten," I tell him. I haul myself up and sit up with my back against the wall, my arms wrapped around my knees. I keep my eyes on my feet.

"I guess I could google it or something," says DJ. "But that would be kind of"—he frowns and scratches his head—"cold, I guess. Was it Karlsen, maybe? Or maybe his first name was Karl. Something like that?"

"Klausen. That's it. Bryan. With a *Y*. I remember now."

It's all there in the newspaper clippings stuffed into the folder under the bed. Out of DJ's reach. I don't want him poring over the clippings.

"Okay. I'll start with Klausen." DJ types, then turns and asks, "Surrey or Delta, do you know? Where he lives?"

"All I remember is that the guy was on his way to pick up his own father to take him for a doctor's appointment."

"Ironic," says DJ. And types some more.

It takes me a couple of seconds to figure out what he means. Then I get it. The man who killed my dad—he was on his way to visit his own dad. Who is still alive, I guess. Part of me wishes *his* father had died. Give him a taste of his own medicine.

But I wouldn't wish that on anyone.

I roll off the bed and swipe my face with a corner of the sheet.

"Eleven Klausens in Surrey and Delta," says DJ. I'm glad he's still got his back to me. "We need more info," he says.

"Cameron!" My sister's voice is followed by the sound of her footsteps on the stairs. Hey, Cam!" Leah bursts into the room. "What're you doing?" She climbs on my bed and bounces a few times. She treats every room like her own personal gym. "Hi, DJ.

What are you guys doing?" she asks again between bounces.

I shoot DJ a look, but he's not even looking my way.

"Leah. Glad you dropped by," he says. "We need to ask you something."

Leah and I speak at the same time. "What?" she asks as I yell, "No!" The last thing I need is DJ saying anything to set the brat off bawling about Dad. Or letting on what we're up to.

When I kick the desk chair, it spins around so hard DJ almost falls off.

"What the heck?" he yells.

Leah bounces harder on the bed, like it's a trampoline or something. "Ask me anything, I bet I know the answer," she says. "Hey. Is this my CD?" she grabs it and starts bouncing again. "It's my Raffi. Ask me a question. Go on, DJ. Make it a hard one."

I hold my breath.

"What should you use to wash an elephant?" DJ asks.

I sigh with relief.

DJ knows Leah well enough that he's not surprised when she answers his dumb question with one of her own. "Why would I need to wash an elephant?"

DJ clears the screen. "Murphy's Oil Soap," he tells her. "You know. The stuff people use to polish furniture. And the why of it is…beats me. I musta read it somewhere."

"Hey, what about a snack?" DJ asks. He might be trying to distract Leah. Or he has a short attention span.

But maybe he's just hungry.

It doesn't matter which. I don't want her to know what we're planning. Whatever that might be.

## Chapter Five

After a few days of thinking about this Klausen guy, I am seriously spooked. I'm suspicious of every back disappearing around a corner. When someone calls with a wrong number, I figure it can only be him. When Mom tells me we've got a new mailman, I dread getting home from school to see what has dropped through the mail slot.

Whatever this guy is doing, I still don't want to think of it as stalking. There's too much of that in the news—usually men stalking their ex-wives and girlfriends. It's spooky when someone you don't know is on your trail, especially if you don't know why they're following you.

Wouldn't most people want to disappear if they'd killed a kid's father—even if it was an accident?

"Let go of me," whines Leah as I bring her home from ballet one day. "I wanted to walk with Selena." She darts out from under the hand I've got on her shoulder to steer her along the sidewalk.

I let go and grab her hand instead. It's as light as a bird, but I'm not letting go. "It's not safe for little girls to be out on their own."

"It's not even dark. Let go, Cam! You're hurting me."

I ease up, but just a bit.

"Carry my bag then!" she says as she shoves it at me.

"Carry it yourself." I grab her collar as a pickup comes around the corner. This one is red. The stalker guy's is blue. But people get new cars all the time.

"Cameron. I'm not a baby," whines Leah. "I can walk by myself."

I try to shake myself out if it. Maybe this is what paranoia feels like.

I don't want to freak Leah out. When I let go, she struts away in front of me. I am tempted to put out my foot and give her a good shove. But I'd never hear the end of it. So I let her get far enough ahead that she can swing her ballet bag without thumping me on the leg.

"Mom's home," she says, as she runs past the Honda.

I bend down to inspect the muffler. Another inch, and it will be dragging on the ground.

"You really should get that car checked out," I say as I follow Leah through the back door.

A chill runs down my back when I see who's in the kitchen with Mom.

Across the table from her are two police officers. The one sitting down is a young woman. With all that bullet-proof stuff she's wearing, you might only know it by her gorgeous blond hair. The other cop is a guy. He is standing against the counter, watching his partner scribbling in her notebook.

"Why are the policemen here?" asks Leah. She dumps her bag on the table and leans against Mom.

Mom runs her hand across Leah's hair. "Just asking a few questions. There was a break-in next door."

"Today?" I feel that chill again. And a ghostly whisper in my ear, *Stalker!*

"Last night, very late we think," said the young woman. "We wonder if you heard anything in the night."

"How did they get in?" I ask.

"The downstairs bathroom window," says Mom. She stares at the kitchen wall as if she could see right through it to the neighbor's house. That window's right opposite our basement door.

"Have you checked our place?" I ask.

"I'd know if anyone had broken in," says Mom. "And I told the officers I didn't hear anything unusual last night. What about you?"

"I was asleep," says Leah. "I dreamed I had a pony and we kept it in the backyard. Can we get a pony, Mom?"

"Oh, sure!" I mutter under my breath.

"Let's talk about that later," says Mom, stroking Leah's cheek as she frowns at me.

"What about you?" The lady cop looks up at me. "Anything you know that might help us?"

For a moment I think of mentioning the stalker. But Mom doesn't know about the video store. And maybe she's already forgotten about the driveway.

One paranoid person in the family is enough. I shrug. "Nah. Can't think of anything. Everything's fine here," I say in a voice that's meant to show I'm the man of the house now. I can handle anything.

I wish I believed it.

# Chapter Six

You'd have thought a visit from the cops would make me feel better. At least we're on their radar. Not that anything's about to happen, I tell myself over and over.

But I'm so shaky on Saturday that instead of dropping her off at Selena's to play, I drag Leah along with me to the grocery store. I have to bribe her by saying I'll buy Pop Tarts if she comes.

All the protective instincts I've developed lately are freaking me out.

Shopping was my job even before Dad died. Which means we get stuff Mom might never think of. And sometimes I forget what we really need.

"Have you got the list?" I ask Leah.

She pats her jacket pocket without answering. "Who would you rather be?" she asks as I pull a shopping cart from the rack.

"Who do I have to choose from?" I ask.

Leah shoves between me and the cart. She grabs the handles and wedges her feet up on the crossbars. "Push me. Come on. Would you rather be SpongeBob or Daffy Duck?"

I hate this game. It reminds me of our summer road trips. Mom with the map spread across her knees. Dad wearing his puke-yellow "traveling" sunglasses. Leah next to me in the back, loaded down with coloring books and boxes of apple juice, yanking the buds from my ears to tell me about something she saw out the window.

I might have missed that bear and her cubs crossing the road up near Jasper if it hadn't been for her though.

"Well? Daffy Duck or SpongeBob?" Leah nags.

"I hate them both," I tell her. "Give me someone else to choose from."

One of her dragging feet slows us down. When I kick it, she tucks it back up under the cart. "All right then. What about the Black Stallion or Raffi?"

There's an easy one. Hearing Raffi's songs every day for the past seven years is more than enough for me. So I say the Black Stallion. Leah has been working her way through the series for the last year. Mom or Dad read her a chapter each night. Now it's just Mom. Leah hasn't sucked me in yet.

"You can't just say which," says my bossy sister. "You're supposed to say why. Can we get strawberries?" Before I can answer, she leans sideways to grab them from the display.

"Gimme the list," I tell her.

She takes one hand off the cart to dig in her pocket. Then switches to the other. "It's gone."

"Outside, you told me you had it."

She tips her head back to look at me. "I just remembered. It was in the other jacket." It took my sister three tries to decide what to wear this morning. At seven, she's already like those prissy girls at school agonizing over their hair and their nails. Like anyone notices.

"Well, you'd better remember what you wrote on it," I tell her. Her printing is crap anyway. We'd never have been able to read it.

"Cap'n Crunch. Marshmallows. Cheese strings. Hawaiian Punch. Fish sticks. Builder Bob spaghetti…" She would keep going, but I lean forward and shove her up tight against the frame of the shopping cart.

"Ouch! Why'd you do that?"

"Get real. That's a fantasy list, and you know it."

"Well, I forget," whines Leah.

"You'd better remember what Mom told you to write down pretty quick," I tell her. I haul a bag of potatoes into the cart and lob in some onions. When I grab a head of broccoli, Leah squeals, "Eew! Mom didn't tell us to get that."

I pull a plastic bag from the roll and shove the broccoli inside. "Well, I love it."

"That's a lie."

"Mom likes it then."

"You just picked broccoli to be mean."

I put one foot on the bottom rung and steer around a corner at a killer angle. I guess it's childish. But DJ and I still fantasize about breaking into a store after dark and having shopping cart races up the aisles.

I'm going so fast, I have to swerve around a guy in the coffee aisle who is taking down one jar after another, reading the labels. I edge past him and watch him sideways while I pull down a can of Mom's brand.

"I want hot chocolate," says Leah. She darts under my arm and grabs a can.

"That's strawberry." As I put it back on the shelf, the man stands aside. He looks at me. Then he turns away.

I grab Leah with one hand, the cart with the other. "Let's go." I haul them along the aisle.

"Hey, I wanted chocolate!" Leah screeches.

"Not now."

"What's the hurry?"

"Shut up," I hiss. We round the corner to the next aisle. I stop the cart. "Stay here. Don't move."

I sneak around the corner, then dart back. My elbow catches on a couple of cans of beans on a display. They tip over and roll across the floor.

I hold my breath. But the rest of the pile holds.

"What's wrong?" Leah's holding a big box of Choconut cereal against her chest.

"Shut up. And put that back," I tell her.

"Why are you being so weird?"

I grab the shopping cart and nudge her with it to get her going up the aisle. "Hop on. Quick."

She dumps the cereal box into the cart and climbs on. We race to the end of the aisle, round the corner and back the way we've just been.

There's no sign of the guy now.

I swing past the shelves of coffee again, getting evil looks from shoppers who have to move out of our way.

"This is fun." Leah's laughing. "Where are we going?"

As I get to the end of the aisle, I turn past the beans again.

Shoppers are pulling stuff off the shelf, checking lists, easing their carts along. An old lady is bending down to grab something from the bottom shelf.

None of them are the guy from the coffee aisle.

The stalker.

Or was it?

I don't know what spooks me out more. That the stalker has followed us to the grocery store. Or that maybe I'm losing my mind.

# Chapter Seven

I patrol the canned-vegetable aisle, checking out everyone and everything.

We cruise up one aisle, then another. I scan the checkouts each time we pass them. I check out the few solo male shoppers.

As I head for the cash register, I think about the kids who grab whatever they want from the shelves and squawk when their mothers make them put it back. From a kid's point of view, Mommy gets everything she wants—laundry powder, toilet paper, vanilla. Lucky Mommy. But the kid can't grab one can of ravioli without having it taken away.

I've only just thought of it like that.

I let Leah grab a can of Builder Bob spaghetti—as if it's any better than the regular spaghetti in tomato sauce that tastes like puke.

"You forgot cookies," whines Leah. Now that we're no longer racing around the store like maniacs, she's bored.

But my heart is still thudding in my chest like a fist against a door. Can it be coincidence that that guy who wanted to shovel our driveway and turned up at the video store now shows up here? I flip open my phone to call Mom. But then I change my mind and call DJ instead.

His phone's on voice mail, so I flip mine shut and pocket it.

I head for the checkout, looking in the other lineups to see if the guy's there.

"Where are we going?" asks Leah. "Did we finish already? Mom said oil. I remember now. And ground beef. Cam!"

I lean across the cart and stick my face into hers. "Will you please shut it? We'll come back later."

"Mom will be mad," she says. "You can't blame me if we didn't get everything. It's not my fault."

"Will you kindly button it," I tell her. "And get off now." I start stacking groceries on the checkout counter. "Help me unload."

"I'm going to tell Mom," Leah says, her bottom lip quivering.

I ignore her and grab her Choconuts from the cart and add them to the pile on the counter.

When I look up, the guy from the coffee aisle is walking out of the store. "Hey! Stop!" I yell. It must be him. The same coat. The same height. That same walk.

Or almost.

I take off with Leah right behind me. "Cam! Where are you going? What about the groceries?"

"Forget about the groceries." I reach back and grab her arm. "Stick with me."

"You're going too fast."

I dart around an old lady pushing a walker and dodge a couple holding hands.

"Hey, you! Hold on a minute," I yell to the guy's back.

When he bends down to get in his car, I realize it's not the same guy. This guy's got a beard.

Crap. I stand in the middle of the lot, wondering what to do next.

I'm not ready to quit, although I have no idea what I'd do to the guy—say to him—if I do catch him.

If only DJ were here. He's never stuck for what to say. He'd know what to do.

But he's not here. "Stay here, okay?" I push Leah against the cart rack between two parking stalls. "Don't move. I will be right back for you."

"What about the groceries?"

"Forget the groceries. And don't you dare move."

# Chapter Eight

I dart between cars, dodging one way and then the other. He must be here. The stalker. I swear that was him in the store.

I peer through windshields and side windows. My head is spinning as I look one way, then the other, at a shadow, someone passing, a movement, any movement.

*So this is what paranoia feels like*, I think as I stand panting and wondering what to do next.

"Hold on there."

The guy marching toward me is wearing a navy and yellow uniform. A rent-a-cop! A badge on his shoulder says Prestige Security. I always figure security guards are wannabe soldiers who can't get into the real army. They'd rather be in Iraq or Afghanistan instead of some crummy grocery store. They all have an overdeveloped sense of their own importance.

Pretending not to have heard him, I turn and look back at Leah. She's climbed on top of the shopping-cart rack and is looking for me in the wrong direction.

"You want to tell me what's going on?" asks the guard.

"I'm looking for my little sister."

"She drive, does she?"

"Course not."

"Or maybe you forgot what your own car looks like." He peers at me. "You're hardly old enough to drive, I'd reckon."

I feel a sudden flush of anger in my chest. Who does he think does the chores that my mother doesn't have time for? How does he think I manage to get the week's groceries home?

Instead of getting into it with him, I take a breath. "You've got it wrong. My sister is a handful. She has a nasty habit of looking for cars that are open," I tell him. "She hides in them. It scares me and my mom to death."

He tips his hat back on his head and scratches his cheek. "So where is your mother then?"

"She's not here right now. It's just me and my sister." I pretend to be scanning the parking lot. I do a phony double take when my eyes land on the cart rack.

Leah's still there. But now she's swinging from the overhead bar like it's a jungle gym.

"Leah!" I use the kind of voice that's meant to show, *Thank goodness I found you. I was so worried.* "There she is," I tell the security guy. "I'd better grab her before she takes off again."

When he puts out one arm toward me, I step out of reach. But it turns out he's just trying to let a car go by.

"I need a few details," he says, taking a notebook out of his pocket. "Incident report. You know how it goes. Just hang on and let me have your name. I'll have a quick word with your sister too."

"I can tell you everything you need to know, officer." As I say it, I know how dumb I sound. He's a security guard, not a cop. "My name is Jason Burke," I tell him. Jason sits two rows behind me in math and aces every test. Never did like him.

I've got to keep the security guard away from Leah. She's bound to mess things up worse than they are. Another lie comes quickly to my lips. "My sister is retarded." No. That's not the word. "She has serious developmental problems," I say. "We live at 137 Drake Drive." I'm not even sure we have a Drake Drive around here. "Now. If you don't mind, sir. I must get my sister home." I push back my sleeve and make a big deal of looking at my watch. "Time for her medication."

I feel like I'm channeling DJ. He's always making up wild stories on the spot.

The rent-a-cop looks from me to Leah and back again to me. He closes his notebook and puts it back in his pocket. "Well, all right then. That seems to be above board." He adjusts his jacket. "Think twice before you go nosing around parked cars again, son.

You must know how it looks. Now go on. Your sister needs you."

Leah is holding on to the metal bar above the shopping carts with one hand. She's waving at me with the other. Luckily, a car drives by, so only I know she's calling my name—which does not sound a bit like Jason.

"It's nice to know that a special kid like that has someone to look after her. Don't see it that often," the security guard says.

Now I feel bad. Maybe this really is his dream job, making sure cars don't get stolen and people don't get mugged for their groceries. "Thank you, sir. Have a good day, now," I say like a law-abiding citizen.

I weave through the cars until I reach my sister.

"What were you doing with that man? I thought he was going to arrest you," says Leah. "What did you do?"

"You ask too many questions," I say. "Let's go home."

"What about the groceries?"

"I told you not to ask questions. Come on."

A car skims by so close that I feel the moving air against my side. I don't bother to check to see who's driving. I just stare straight ahead as I lead my sister to Mom's old Honda.

I should go back into the store and see if the cart we abandoned is still there. But all my energy has seeped out through my shoes.

I can't keep this to myself anymore.

Whether I want to or not, I have to tell Mom about the stalker. If it is only my imagination and the man of the house is about to lose his mind, she should know.

I find the car and shove Leah in. I hope the muffler doesn't fall off before we get home.

# Chapter Nine

When we get home, Mom is at the kitchen table with yesterday's paper spread in front of her. Behind her, the coffeemaker is gurgling.

"I thought you were at the store," she says, when she sees we're empty-handed.

"We got broccoli for you. And brown spaghetti," says Leah. "But I left the list at home. We couldn't finish the shopping because Cam saw someone and ran out of the store."

"I said I would explain to Mom." I poke Leah in the back. "Okay?"

"Fine then," she says. "Mom, can I watch TV?" Leah leaves the room without waiting for an answer.

Mom folds up the paper and looks up at me. "Explain what, Cam?"

"Remember the guy on the driveway? That day it snowed?" I say. "You want this coffee, or can I have it?"

"Finish it. I'm done. What about the guy on the driveway?" Mom turns to watch me pour the coffee into a mug and add cream and three sugars. Then one more.

I sit down and stack the sections of the paper.

"The guy in the driveway?" Mom prompts me.

"One day he came into the video store," I say. "And he was at Shop Rite just now." I watch her face as I tell her, "I think he's still stalking us."

Mom folds her hands on the table so I won't notice the trembling. "You sure this is the same man?" she asks.

"Pretty sure," I say. "Well, the first time I couldn't be sure. But this time? Yeah. Well maybe. I'm pretty sure it was Bryan Klausen."

Mom shivers. It starts in her shoulders, then runs down her arms.

"He was in the coffee aisle," I say. As if it makes a difference.

Mom's hands are still shaking. "I knew I should have done what I threatened that first time. Get a restraining order." She stands up and pulls her housecoat tight around her. "Why didn't you tell me, Cam? When you saw him at work?"

"Well, like I said, I couldn't be sure."

"But now you are?"

"I don't know I'd swear to it in court. But yes. I think so."

Mom pulls the phone off the wall.

"Mom. It's Saturday. Do the cops handle this kind of thing on the weekend?"

She tips the phone sideways so she can answer me. "I'm not going to call the police. I'm calling Gail. Her husband is a lawyer. He'll know what to do." She punches in the number, then holds the phone against her chest. "God, I wish your father was here."

For a second I think of saying how stupid that is. If Dad was here, the guy wouldn't be stalking us, would he? But one look at her face, and I keep my mouth shut.

I get up and put our mugs in the sink.

Leah bounces into the room. "Who are you calling, Mom?"

"Come on, kid," I tell her. "I'm going to hose down my bike. Wanna do yours?"

She sends a sideways look at Mom, who is listening to the phone with her eyes closed. "What's Mom doing?" asks Leah.

Without answering, I grab my sister's arm and haul her out of the room.

Mom comes outside as I'm emptying the bucket of grubby water into the drain at the end of the driveway. She's wearing her work scrubs now.

"Don't go too far," Mom calls to Leah. She's riding her bike along the sidewalk as fast as she can to dry it off. "You shouldn't let her go off on her own," Mom tells me.

Until six months ago, my bratty sister had the run of the neighborhood. We've lived here so long, it's hard to make a move without everyone knowing about it. But lately even I get nervous when Leah is out of sight, especially if roads and traffic are involved.

"I'm watching her," I say. "So what did Gail's husband say?"

"Lucas said that three sightings is not much to go on. The cops wouldn't do much with it. Me and all my talk about restraining orders." She wraps her arms around herself.

"I think I should talk to the guy," I tell her. "Find out what he wants."

"He told me. I told you. He wants to make up for what he did," Mom tells me. "Offer some support. Some *practical assistance*. His words exactly. Although what he meant..." She shakes her head, like there's stuff in there she'd like to pry loose.

"I just wish he'd bug off," I say. This isn't quite the truth. Part of me wonders what the guy means by practical assistance. We never got much of that from Dad.

"Leah. That's enough now," Mom calls as my sister heads back down the sidewalk. "I wish he'd bug off too," says Mom. "But I'm at a loss as how to make it happen."

"Maybe I should track him down. See if I can get him off our case."

"It's not up to you, Cameron." She puts one hand on my arm. "I'm the parent here. It's my job to keep you and your sister safe."

I shake off her hand and step out of reach. I kick the empty bucket so it rolls away on its side. "So why don't you then?" I'm surprised at the rush of anger that swamps me. "I take care of Leah!" I yell. "I do the groceries. Mow the lawn. The days you are home, you spend sleeping. The rest of the time you're at work. Now suddenly you're going to take care of things?"

"Cam. Don't." She steps toward me.

I step back. "Everyone tells me I'm the man of the family. So I'll take care of this." I am shaking almost as much as Mom had been earlier. Now she's turned to watch Leah. And Leah's watching us. She sits astride her bike, one foot on the sidewalk, the other on a pedal.

"I'll tell him that we don't need him," I say to my mother's back. "What did Dad ever do but bury his head in his books anyway? If we didn't need Dad's help when he was alive, we hardly need this guy's help now."

"Why are you yelling?" Leah watches Mom stomp back into the house. "Why is Mom crying?" She lets her bike drop to the ground. "Everything is horrible!" she shrieks. "All you do is drag me around and bully me and yell at Mom and make us all cry." She pushes past me. "I hate it. I hate Dad. Everything's awful, and I hate you all."

I watch her run into the house calling, "Mom! Mommy, where are you?"

I aim a kick at Leah's bike and watch it scrape sideways across the driveway.

I've still got the car keys in my pocket. I'd like nothing more than to take off and drive until the tank of gas is empty.

I look back at the house. Then, without moving Leah's bike onto the lawn, which would be the responsible thing to do, I open the driver's-side door of the Honda and get in.

As I take off, I check my watch. Mom has to go to work in twenty minutes.

Fine, I think as I pull out onto the road. She can take the bus.

## Chapter Ten

"Where are you off to?" Mom asks DJ and me after breakfast. He came over last night after she left for work. We stayed up all night trying to figure out what to do.

Even though I only drove around the block a couple of times and got the car back in time for Mom to get to work, she's still mad. I don't dare ask for the car today.

"Errands for my father," says DJ. He disappears into the hall before Mom can ask any more questions.

"Can I come? Where are you going?" asks Leah.

I follow DJ out without answering. All the way down the path, we can still hear her screeching in the house.

As we head toward the bus stop, he asks, "So, you got the address?"

I shove back my sleeve. It's written on my arm. I didn't want to write it on a piece of paper that blabbermouth Leah could find. "Errands for your father?" I say. "That's pretty lame."

He ducks his head. "Actually, I did say I'd pick up some WD-whattzit for him."

I don't say anything. I don't know the last time DJ offered to do anything for his old man.

"Come on!" We dash to the bus stop and manage to climb aboard before the driver closes the doors.

I collapse in a seat behind a mother whose snotty baby is climbing all over her. DJ drops down beside me. "You figured out the route?"

"Two buses," I tell him. "I MapQuested it. Thought about what we're going to do when we get there, Sherlock?"

"Hey, this is your gig, man. But I say we check things out. Get ourselves noticed."

Two girls our age get on the bus. They are wearing almost identical clothes, tight jeans and skinny tops. They're both talking loudly on cell phones. I wouldn't be surprised if they were yakking to each other.

DJ leers at them.

The girls ignore him as they sidle past the woman's baby buggy. "So, like,

I said if she was going to keep it up, she could think again," says the one in the pink shirt.

"I told you I'd be home by six…I'll be home by six," says the other, obviously to her mother. Or father.

I open my cell. No messages. I'm just about to pocket it again, when it rings. Home phone. I debate whether to answer it. Then hit Talk. Mom's mad enough at me already. "Yeah?"

"I know where you're going," says Leah. "I'm going to tell Mom."

I've told her not to call me on my cell. "Where am I going, smarty pants?" I make a face at DJ.

He mouths, "The brat?"

I nod. "We're going to Home Depot for DJ's dad," I tell Leah.

"You're going to meet that man. I heard you and DJ talking. I'll tell Mom."

"I told you. We're going to the mall. Want me to bring you something?" I ask. "A treat?"

DJ rolls his eyes at me and turns in his seat to ogle the girls, who are now too busy texting to notice him.

"I want that new Miley Cyrus CD," says Leah.

"I mean candy, idiot. Something like that. Look. I gotta go."

"I'll tell."

"I'll bring pizza. How about we have pizza for supper?" I ask.

She knows when she's being bribed. "You're not going to Home Depot, are you?"

"See you later." I hang up.

"She onto you?" DJ asks.

"Probably." I shrug. I hope Leah keeps her mouth shut, pizza or no pizza. I can imagine what Mom will say if she finds out we're stalking the guy who's stalking us.

But this isn't stalking. It's a stakeout.

Even if I have no idea what to do when we got there.

## Chapter Eleven

Bryan Klausen lives in an ordinary house. A blue Ford pickup is parked outside. A green hose is curved under one tire. The driveway is shiny wet. A bucket sits in the middle of a flower bed full of orange flowers. Maybe he's been washing bikes with his kids.

"So, the plan?" asks DJ.

I am looking at the basketball hoop attached to the garage wall. There's one just like it outside our house. It was there when we moved in. I've played there with my friends, but my dad would no more shoot hoops than he'd take ballet classes.

I imagine Bryan Klausen playing basketball with his kids. Maybe right now they are inside playing a board game together.

I bet Bryan Klausen doesn't spend hours in his dusty study, poring over economic reports. I bet he doesn't look up, dazed and frowning, when someone calls him to supper, asks for a ride or for help hooking up a new stereo.

I'm about to tell DJ that we should split when the front door opens.

I grab his arm and spin him around so we're facing back up the road.

"Hey! What's up?" he says.

"He might see us."

"I thought that was the point." He pulls out of my grip and turns back. "Looks like he's going jogging."

All I see is a guy in shorts and a long-sleeved T-shirt moving at quite a clip.

"Come on. But not too close," says DJ. He takes off after the guy, who may or may not be Bryan Klausen. "Catch me if you can," he taunts me.

It doesn't take me long.

The jogger ahead has a nice smooth stride. But we've not gone half a block before DJ is panting. He runs like a windmill, his legs and arms flailing around. I'm not much better, but I know to keep my arms close to my sides.

The guy we're following—my dad's killer—jogs in place while he waits for a truck to pass at the intersection. Then he crosses without missing a beat.

"Guy's. Wearing. An iPod," pants DJ. His elbow jabs me as I move closer to hear.

"So?" I ask.

"He. Won't. Know. We're. Behind him. Can't hear." When he stops and leans back with his fists on his hips, I see sweat on DJ's brow. "I can't keep up," he says between breaths. "In fact, I may be having a heart attack."

"You're out of shape." I don't tell him that the stitch in my side feels like someone's shoved a knife in there. I pretend I'm not as out of breath as he is.

I scan the street. The guy's disappeared. "Crap."

"What?" When DJ looks up, his face is red.

"We lost him," I say.

"Good. I don't think I could keep that up much longer. Let's grab something to eat and wait to see if he comes back this way."

We've stopped in front of a Subway. Inside, DJ orders a meatball footlong.

I grab a cookie and a pop. We sit at the counter against the window, looking outside.

"Did you see *Casino Royale*?" A piece of onion sticks out of DJ's mouth as he munches. The sub's down to six inches already.

"What's wrong with you?" I ask. "We saw it together."

"Was that a stuntman, do you think?" he asks. "The opening sequence? Or Daniel Whatzzit himself?"

"I read about it somewhere. All that running, jumping. It's got a name. A French word. Some French guy invented it. Almost like a martial art."

"Think there's someplace to learn it?" asks DJ. He laughs. "We might need it, if we keep checking out your guy." He crams the last of his sandwich into his mouth and crumples up the paper.

"He's just jogging, for crying out loud."

"He got away from you though. Didn't he?"

I could give him a smart-ass answer to that. But what's the point?

"What say we head back to his house and hang out across the street?" DJ asks. "He'll come back."

"Then what?"

"How 'bout this?" he asks. He spins his stool as he stands up. "How about a sign of some kind. We'll write on his driveway. Or leave a note stuck under his windshield. Something like…What could we say?"

"*We know who you are*?" I suggest.

"How about, *You are being watched*? That should spook him."

We're outside when the jogger— Bryan Klausen—sprints by. I know it's him.

He's holding a newspaper under one arm and a plastic Safeway bag in his other hand. They don't seem to slow him down.

DJ pulls me back against the storefront. Once the guy's a little way ahead, DJ starts running.

I follow. But there's no rush. We know where he's going.

# Chapter Twelve

It's hard to be inconspicuous staking out the stalker's house. We're sitting on the ground, leaning against a short wall across the street. A couple of leaves drift down from the tree overhead.

The blue pickup truck is still in the driveway. The bucket is still in the flower bed. No one has picked up the hose.

I try to get comfortable on the hard ground and imagine what might be going on inside Bryan Klausen's house. Beside me, DJ throws his hacky sack in the air over and over.

I try to remember what the papers said about Klausen. In my head I run through everything I can recall from the article.

Newspapers think they're telling you the whole story. But it's just information that isn't even interesting. Even when it's stuck together to make a story, they're bound to miss what really went on.

The papers didn't mention that my dad probably wasn't looking where he was going when he stepped out into traffic. There was no mention of the faraway look on his face when he was thinking about financial forecasts. He would disappear into his thoughts about numbers while he was eating dinner or driving the car—or jogging.

The newspaper article said nothing about the maple syrup Leah insisted she have on her pancakes, even though Mom said she should make do with jam.

Was it Leah's fault that Dad dashed out of the house to pick up syrup for her French toast? Was it Mom's fault for insisting that Dad be responsible for one meal a week? Or that all he ever made were pancakes? Was it my fault for sleeping late and not doing the errand instead of Dad? I'd forgotten to pick up maple syrup at the store the week before—even though it was on the list.

Was it Bryan Klausen's fault for being on the same road, headed to see his own dad, when my father ran out between two cars without looking?

I reach out and grab the hacky sack midair. "This is stupid." I stand up and start walking.

DJ dashes after me. "What's stupid?"

"This stakeout, or whatever you call it.

"You thought it was a good idea last night. Give me back that sack."

"Only if you keep it in your pocket." I toss it to him as I get up to leave. I can't get away from this house fast enough.

He's having a hard time keeping up with me. "What's the hurry? Where are you going now? I thought…"

"Forget it. Just forget it," I say. I jog around the next corner and cross the street with DJ on my heels.

"Slow down, man. Did we come all this way just to have a sub and stare at a guy's house?"

I stop and turn to face him. "I'm going home." It's probably all in my head anyway. "You coming or not?" I ask.

"I wish you'd make up your mind," DJ says. He shoves his hands in his pockets. "So, you coming with me to Home Depot? It's on the way."

We spend most of the afternoon at DJ's house, oiling everything in sight, whether it needs it or not.

# Chapter Thirteen

Monday is Mom's day off. She lets me take the car to school on the condition that I pick up Leah on the way home.

Neither of us has mentioned my tantrum on the driveway the other day.

With fifteen minutes to kill before Leah's school lets out, I pull into the curb and text DJ to see if he's home yet. I laugh when he texts back, *GTG GIMS*.

GIMS is DJ's code for Girl in My Sights. And his answer to my question, *Stacie?*, is just another *GTG*.

As I close my phone and lean over to pull my binder from the backseat, I see a guy walking up and down the sidewalk. He looks like just an ordinary guy from where I'm sitting.

But everyone knows stalkers look like regular people.

The cluster of moms with baby buggies watches him for a minute, then ignores him.

I open my homework. Without Dad's help, my grades in math and science are bottoming out. Mom won't let me drop Math 11, even though I swear I have no plans to be a doctor or a scientist. Or an economist.

When I look up from my trig questions, the same guy is still pacing in front of the school, his head down. The gang of mothers is bigger now.

The crosswalk lady is talking to them, her Stop sign propped on the sidewalk beside her.

I close my binder and throw it in the back of the car. I roll the window down to get a closer look.

With all the newspaper stories about predators around school grounds, why aren't these parents paying attention? What good is that woman in her stupid yellow uniform if she's not doing her job? Doesn't anyone care who's lurking around the school waiting for kids to come out so they can grab one?

How's that for paranoia?

The guy looks around, then wanders across the grass toward a classroom window.

Leah's classroom.

I feel as if a cold hand has grabbed the back of my neck. I belt out of the car and charge after him.

He ducks around the corner toward the side door.

I knew I should have confronted the guy when I had the chance.

An echoey mix of footsteps and voices drifts out of the building. Does Leah have gym last class on Mondays? Or Tuesdays? I can't think straight.

The guy is almost at the side door now. I'm 90 percent sure this is Bryan Klausen. Maybe 80 percent. It's that 10- or 20-percent chance of being wrong that makes me hesitate. Some math is not so hard to figure out.

As the man takes the first step that leads to the gym, the school buzzer goes. Within seconds, the doors are flung open and a crowd of kids flood the playground.

I scan their faces looking for Leah, at the same time trying to keep my eye on the guy.

"Hi, Cam." It's Selena. "Leah fell off the bars, but she's okay—"

I grab her. "Where is she?"

"That hurts!" Selena pulls away and rubs her shoulder. "I was just saying…"

"I know. I know. I'm sorry." I reach out to touch where I grabbed her, but she trots off. "I gotta go. I have piano. Tell Leah I'll see her tomorrow." She looks at me sideways as she goes, as if she's scared of me suddenly.

I clench my teeth in frustration as I watch to check that her mom's there to meet her. Then I turn to look for my sister. And the stalker, the man who might not be the stalker.

He is gone.

I feel panicky breath rise in my chest. Is he inside? Did he get to her first? "Leah!"

A huddle of kids step out of my way as I charge into the building.

I look like a crazy person as I head down the hallway, past the library, the girls' washroom and the grade-six room.

"Leah!" I yell as I dash past empty classrooms.

A teacher sticks his head out of a doorway. Mr. Phillips. "Cameron Gifford, isn't it?"

I skid to a stop and feel the sweat prickle my neck.

"It's been a while. Looking for Leah, I hear." He smiles. "I did enjoy having her in my class last year." As opposed to the pain I was, I expect he's thinking. "Do you and Derek still pal around?" he asks.

"DJ and I hang out a bit." I don't have time for this. "Have you seen Leah?"

"In the health office. Just a bump, I think. She said you'd be here to pick her up."

I dash off. I don't answer when he calls after me to ask how Mom is doing.

Leah is sitting on the examination table, kicking her feet against it. "Wanna see my bump?" she asks.

"Was there a guy here?"

"What guy? Ms. Lonsdale said to wait here. She'll be right back. You have to sign something. Wanna see my bump?" she asks again.

There's no bump that I can see. But her forehead is sweaty.

I hug her.

She pulls away. "What's that for?" she asks.

I drop my arms. "I'm just glad you're safe."

"Course I'm safe. But I did climb up as far as the sixth rung on the wall bars. It was a long way to fall. Can we go home?"

"You said we had to wait for Ms. Lonsdale."

I look around the room. Everything seems so calm. So normal. But my breath is burning my throat, and my skin is clammy with fear.

Something's not right.

I check the hallway. Leah's teacher is coming my way, holding a clipboard. Walking in the other direction is a guy holding hands with two kids, one on each side. This almost looks normal too.

But it could be the guy from outside. I clench my teeth in frustration.

"Are there any kids called Klausen in your school?" I ask Leah.

"I don't know. I've never heard of them." She's peering at the nutrition chart on the wall. "Can we go home now? Have you got Mom's car?"

I feel my breath slowing. My blood is cooling as I watch Ms. Lonsdale smooth my sister's hair across her forehead. "You can go home when Cam has signed this form." She hands me the clipboard and a pen. "This says that we're releasing Leah into your care, and you will monitor her condition." She smiles at me.

I sign the paperwork with a hand that is almost steady. I pass it back.

When I reach out to take Leah's hand, she steps aside. "I'm not a baby, you know."

Her teacher smiles at me and pats Leah on the shoulder. "Off you go. You'll survive."

"Bye, Ms. Lonsdale." Leah skips down the hall ahead of me.

I keep my eyes open as we head back outside. I look around as we get into the car. The group of mothers has broken up. The schoolyard is almost empty.

There's no sign of the suspicious-looking guy.

I'm not sure now that there was anything to be suspicious about. Except that any minute I might lose my mind. One more thing for my family to deal with.

I lean my head against the steering wheel and close my eyes.

"Cam?" Leah asks.

"What?'

"Can we stop at Timmy's for a donut?"

I turn to look at her.

"Can we?" she says.

I want to reach out and touch her. Hug her. Keep her safe forever.

But I just say, "Yes. Then I'm dropping you off at home. There's something I have to do."

# Chapter Fourteen

I sit in the car across from Klausen's house and bite my lip as I dial my cell, hoping DJ will pick up.

I'm calm now, calmer than I've been for days. Now I know what to do. And I'm the only one who can do it.

When DJ answers, I tell him, "I'm going to talk to the guy before I lose my mind."

"Where are you?"

"Outside his house."

"You're not going to bail like you did last time?"

"Not a chance." I can't see movement at Klausen's house. "No way. I'm up for this," I say. But I'm not sure I am up for it.

"You okay going in there alone?"

"You make it sound like I'm advancing on Baghdad," I tell him. "Didn't you hear me say I want to do this?"

I don't know what I want. Yes, I do. I want the movie of my life to rewind. I want it to stop on that frame with me, my mom and dad and my sister sitting around the kitchen table stabbing pancakes with our forks.

But it's too late. This movie only goes one way.

"You wanna wait for me?" DJ asks. "I can head right over."

"Maybe not."

His voice is flooded with relief. "If you're sure…"

"Yeah. I'm sure."

"So what are you going to say?" he asks.

"Beats me." I laugh nervously.

"You'll think of something." I can tell he's losing interest. "Later, then," he says. "And good luck, dude."

I sit for a minute looking at my phone before I ram it in my pocket. I get out of the car, lock it and cross the street.

I stab at the doorbell before I can change my mind.

I hear a man inside call, "I'll get it." The door opens.

Bryan Klausen is wearing a sports coat and tie and is holding a mug.

What had the guy at Leah's school been wearing?

"Yes?"

I can tell he recognizes me by the way he steps back. "Oh my god…"

I realize I've got my hand out to shake his, like I'm a civilized person. I pull it back and stick it in my pocket. "I'm Cameron Gifford," I tell him. I clear my throat. "You've been following me."

He looks down the hallway. He turns toward me again. "Look. Can we… I don't want to talk here. My wife…"

I thought I was the paranoid one.

"I need to talk to you," I say. I hope he can't hear the quiver in my voice.

"Of course you do." He peers past me and nods toward the garage door, which is gaping open.

I look inside at the loaded shelves and a bicycle lying on its side.

"We can talk in there." He turns away from me again. "I'll be right back, Lynne," he calls down the hallway.

Inside the garage, he looks into his mug, then sets it down on a shelf. "How did you find me?" he asks.

"Probably the same way you found me."

"Your address was in the police report," he tells me.

"Yours wasn't," I say. "But Canada411 worked."

He nods. "Yes. Of course." He folds his arms across his chest. "What do you want?"

What's wrong with this guy? He shows up on our driveway, tracks me down at work, follows me at the grocery store. He shows up at Leah's school.

Then he acts like *I'm* behaving strangely.

"I could ask you the same," I say.

Klausen pushes his hand through his hair. He sighs. His voice trembles as he says, "I've tried over and over again to think how I can make it up to you and your family."

I study the pile of games stacked on one of the shelves. Sorry is in the middle of the pile. Leah loves Sorry.

I turn back to face him. "You thought you could make it up to us? You ran down my dad like he was some bug."

His face pales. "It was an accident."

"Yes. I know. But he's still dead, isn't he?"

He nods. "He is. And if I could…" Tears tremble on his eyelids.

"Don't you dare say that if you could bring him back, you would. At least say something original!"

He glances toward the door that leads into the house.

"Why are we talking out here?" I ask.

"My wife doesn't know."

"Doesn't know what? How could she not know?" I'm almost yelling now. I don't care who hears.

He's almost whispering when he answers. "She doesn't know that I tried to make contact with your family. And if she did..." He looks down at his shoes, then back at me. "Tell me about your dad," he pleads. "I'd like to know about him."

# Chapter Fifteen

I step back. "Why do you want me to tell you about my dad?"

Bryan Klausen shrugs. "Maybe if I had a better sense of him…"

"You'd feel better? Is that what you think?" I don't care about his wife, but I'm not shouting anymore. "How will knowing about the man you killed make you feel better?"

I watch him shrink into himself. "I don't know." He sounds tired. "It might help me figure out what I can do to make up for what I did."

"You can't," I say. "Don't you get it?"

He frowns at me and bites his lip.

"You can't make up for what you did," I say again.

"But there must be something. I don't know. Household stuff. Take you out to a hockey game. You like hockey? I could fix your car. Sounds like that muffler needs replacing."

I shove my hands in my pocket and watch his mouth move. Maybe if I let him go on long enough, he will hear how outrageous he sounds.

Or maybe he will start to make sense to me.

"There must be stuff your mom needs help with," he goes on with desperation in his voice. "The yard work, maybe. You've got a big yard. I thought that if

I could talk to you, I could find out what kind of help you might need."

"We don't need your help."

"Well, perhaps…"

"Mr. Klausen." I step forward again. "My dad never fixed the car or mowed the lawn in his life. He hated hockey. I take out the garbage. Mom mows the lawn. My dad?" I swallow to hold back the tears. "He built some shelves once. In my sister's closet. As soon as he was done, he closed the door and they all fell down. That was the last time my father did anything useful in the house." It's a joke at home. I'm surprised to find myself almost smiling at the memory. "There's nothing to help us with," I tell him.

"Maybe I…"

"There's nothing you can do for us. Nothing." I lower my voice when I see him glance nervously at the door. "Except one thing."

He leans toward me eagerly.

"Leave us alone."

"But…" There are tears on his cheeks.

I feel tears trailing down mine. I shake my head. I lean toward him. "Mr. Klausen," I say. "It was an accident. I know that. But my father is gone. For good. Get it?"

Klausen leans farther back against the freezer with every word, as if I'm giving him a good shove.

"But you know what?" I continue. "My dad was not much use for anything at all. Except being the person he was. I miss him. My mom misses him. My sister misses him." I step back and wrap my arms around myself. "You want to feel better about what happened," I tell him. "That's *your* problem. We can't help you with it."

"You're right," he says quietly. "I'm sorry."

I look around at the games stacked on the shelves and the row of paint cans on the windowsill. Below the window is a huge toolbox, the tall kind with wheels. I bet Bryan Klausen has all the right tools to fix a muffler.

"Maybe you are sorry. I am too," I tell him. "But you have to leave me alone. Leave my family alone."

He doesn't look so sinister anymore. And now I'm not sure he was stalking us. What if it hadn't been him at the grocery store? Or the school?

It was him in my driveway though. He introduced himself to my mom. But the rest of the time?

Maybe it doesn't matter.

Bryan Klausen is nodding slowly. "You're right. Of course. You're right."

"Mr. Klausen," I tell him. "If I ever suspect that you've been following me, or my family, I will report you to the police." My voice is strong and steady.

"Of course. Yes. Look…I have to tell you…"

"I'm done here." I walk out of the garage into the bright sunlight, before Klausen can say any more—before I can say any more.

Before I feel any sorrier for the guy than I do already.

# Chapter Sixteen

A letter arrives this morning. A business letter, by the looks of it.

Mom doesn't notice it at first. She's studying the real-estate flyer. "We might think about moving," she says, flipping the pages. "Wouldn't you like to live in a place that's not so full of Dad's memories?"

"I don't mind them," I tell her. And I realize that I mean it. "They're all that's left of him."

She looks at me over the top of her glasses. Like Dad used to.

I almost laugh.

"Maybe later then," she says. "We'll give ourselves a little longer." She folds the flyer in half twice.

I watch her do it a third time. Then I say, "Did you know it's only possible to fold any piece of paper in half seven times?"

"Your dad could have explained why." It's the first time I've heard Mom talk about him without tearing up.

She picks up the letter, turns it over, then looks at the front again. "It's from a lawyer," she tells me. "Not ours though. Ambulance chaser probably."

"Ambulance chaser?"

"There are lawyers that track down people who've lost a family member. Itching to take someone to court. Make lots of money." She grimaces. She tears open the envelope and takes out the letter. She reads it and turns it over. When she sees that the back of the page is blank, Mom reads the front again. With each movement, her face gets paler.

Finally I ask, "What is it?"

"Hang on a minute." She closes her eyes and leans back in her chair. When she opens them again, she puts the letter on the table. "Make me a coffee, would you? Instant will do."

The letter stays on the table while I fill the kettle and take Mom's mug from the cupboard. Then I reach to the back and pull out Dad's. Stenciled on it are the words, *Of course I have problems. I'm an economist.*

When I bring our drinks to the table, Mom is reading the letter again.

She hands it to me. "What do you think?" she asks. "Is this weird or what?"

Mom blows on her coffee to cool it while I read the letter. It's written in lawyer-ish language. A trust fund has been set up in the names of Leah and Cameron Gifford in the amount of $25,000. It is to be used for our post-secondary education.

"Twenty-five thou," I mutter.

"It's not that much, really," says Mom. "Not with the cost of school these days."

The benefactor has asked that his or her name be withheld, the letter says. But I can guess. "The stalker," I say.

Mom frowns. "You think so? The man who killed your father?" I don't answer. She's talking to herself. She doesn't touch the letter. "Who else could it be?"

"It's Bryan Klausen," I say. "I'm pretty sure. Sounds like something he would do."

Mom squints at me. "How would you know?"

"I met him a couple of weeks ago," I tell her.

"You did what?" She leans toward me.

"I met him."

"Where? How?"

"I went to his house," I say.

"After I told you I would take care of it?"

"It was the only way to get things straightened out."

"Straightened out." Mom's jaw is clenching and unclenching. I imagine her teeth grinding together.

"I told you. He showed up at work. At the grocery store." I don't know why I don't tell her about Leah's school. Maybe because I don't want to let on how paranoid I have been.

In a quiet voice, Mom asks, "And did you get things straightened out?"

"I told him that he couldn't do anything to make us feel better about what happened to Dad. And we couldn't make him feel better. That's what it was all about—shoveling the driveway. He thought he could help with stuff Dad would be doing if he was still around."

"Shows how much he knew about your father." She takes a deep breath and closes her eyes.

"I know. I told the poor guy about those shelves in Leah's room."

Mom smiles. "Did you now?" She starts to laugh. It's a real laugh that comes from deep in her chest.

She tips back her head and roars.

I feel the heat of tears in my eyes as I wait for my mother's laughter to change to crying. But she just laughs and laughs.

When she's finished, she walks around the table. She pulls me against her.

"I figure it was about him," I say, my voice muffled in her side. "Him needing to feel better. Bryan Klausen. The stalker. He really feels bad."

Mom sits down again and picks up the letter. She folds it against her chest. "I imagine he does." She flaps the letter against the table edge.

"What will you do?" I ask. "About the trust fund?

"It's not up to me."

"We could use it," I tell her.

She shakes her head. "We don't need it."

A beat behind, without knowing I'm going to say it, I tell her, "I don't think we should take it."

Mom nods. "Fine. Good. I'll write the lawyer. Ask him to thank his client. Maybe one day…do you have his number?"

"Isn't it on the letter?" I ask.

"Not the lawyer. Bryan Klausen's number."

For a moment I think of lying. Instead, I nod.

"Maybe you should call him. Thank him. Say no thanks." She ducks her head, then looks at me again. "Do you like him?"

"He's just a guy, Mom."

Bryan Klausen does not belong in my life. It doesn't matter what he has in his toolbox. No one can replace my father, however good of a Mr. Fix-It he might be.

"Write to the lawyer," I tell Mom. "Let the lawyer thank him. I won't be phoning him."

She looks at me for a long moment but doesn't argue. She refolds the letter. "What shall we tell Leah?"

"How about we don't tell her anything?" I answer. "Think what she'd want to do with twenty-five grand. All those Miley Cyrus CDs!"

"But don't you think we need to tell this…Bryan that he should stay away?

Do I need to mention an injunction again?"

"He won't be back, Mom."

She thinks for a moment, then nods. "If you say so." She slides the letter back into its envelope. She takes our mugs to the sink and, with her back to me, says, "Have I told you how much help you've been? I couldn't have survived the last six months without you taking up the slack."

I don't tell her it's been seven months since Dad died.

I get up and stand beside her at the sink. I pick up dad's mug. I rinse and dry it. I put it near the front of the cupboard, where I can reach it next time.

It's weeks before I stop looking over my shoulder. Even though I don't really expect to see Bryan Klausen again. I can't even be sure it was him all those times I thought he was stalking us.

It doesn't matter now.

I still walk Leah to school, take her to ballet and keep close tabs on her. Not because I'm paranoid. But as my grandmother reminds me every time she calls, I'm the man of the house now.

On our way home from Shop Rite one Saturday, I take the car in and get a quote on a new muffler.

# Acknowledgments

With many thanks to all the folks at Orca for their support, input and skills that combine to provide such a warm and welcoming home for my work. Thanks especially to Melanie Jeffs, for her fine editorial eye.

Lois Peterson wrote for adults for more than twenty years before she started writing novels for younger readers in 2007. This is her fourth book for Orca Book Publishers, following *Meeting Miss 405*, *The Ballad of Knuckles McGraw* and *Silver Rain*. She lives in Surrey, British Columbia, where she works for a public library and teaches creative writing to children, teens and adults. Check out her website at www.loispeterson.net.

# orca currents

For more information on all the books
in the Orca Currents series, please visit
**www.orcabook.com**